DAVID AND GOLIATH

Beatrice Schenk de Regniers

illustrated by Scott Cameron

ORCHARD BOOKS   NEW YORK

David and Goliath

has many meanings for me. I wanted to tell the story, keeping the strength and glory of the biblical language and at the same time following a prototype of the folktale in which the youngest son, through his fearlessness and his innocence, conquers evil—and wins the hand of the princess, too. And because I have always found great pleasure in the Psalms, I was happy to find that they wove themselves into the story.

Orchard Books, 95 Madison Avenue, New York, NY 10016

Manufactured in the United States of America. Printed by Barton Press, Inc. Bound by Horowitz/Rae. Book design by Jean Krulis. The text of this book is set in 12 point Palatino. The illustrations are oil paintings reproduced in full color.

1   3   5   7   9   10   8   6   4   2

Library of Congress Cataloging-in-Publication Data
De Regniers, Beatrice Schenk. David and Goliath / Beatrice Schenk de Regniers ;
illustrated by Scott Cameron.   p.   cm.
Summary: The biblical tale of the young shepherd who uses a slingshot to do battle with a giant
and eventually becomes a king.
ISBN 0-531-09496-0.—ISBN 0-531-08796-4 (lib. bdg.)
1. David, King of Israel—Juvenile literature.   2. Goliath (Biblical giant)—Juvenile literature.
3. Bible stories, English—O.T. Samuel, 1st.   [1. David, King of Israel.   2. Goliath (Biblical giant)
3. Bible stories—O.T.]   I. Cameron, Scott, ill.   II. Title.
BS580.D3D39   1996   222'.4309505—dc20   95-22025

This book is for my brother
Daniel X.
—B.S.deR.

For Johanna Deignan
—S.C.

There was a farmer in Bethlehem in the land of Israel, and he had seven sons. The six eldest sons were full-grown men, tall and strong—taller than their father and stronger. And often they made fun of their youngest brother, David, who was only a lad, and small for his age at that.

Whenever David asked to go hunting with his brothers, or to join them in their work or in their fun, they scornfully refused.

Eliab, the eldest brother, would say, "Go, little David, and sing to your father's sheep, and play your little harp. And shoot at flies with your little slingshot. Truly, that is all you are good for."

Then David would take up his shepherd's staff and bring his father's sheep to graze on the hillside. Over one shoulder he carried his harp, and over the other his shepherd's bag. And in one hand he carried his slingshot. On his way, he gathered the smoothest pebbles he could find and put them in his shepherd's bag.

While he watched his father's sheep, David sat under a fig tree and played his harp so sweetly and so gaily that the lambs danced and skipped in the meadow. Even the ewes and the old rams skipped and danced in their grave fashion.

Then David looked at the blue sky and at the little green hills, and up to the great mountains beyond the hills. And it seemed to David that even the mountains were skipping like rams, and the hills were dancing and skipping like lambs to his music.

David was so happy, he made up a song of praise. He sang of lambs and rams and hills and mountains dancing and skipping in praise of the Lord. And David forgot his brothers' scorn.

But one day when David came back to the farmhouse, he found his elder brothers had gone off to be soldiers in King Saul's army. For the king's enemies, the Philistines, were gathering together their army to fight King Saul and his men of Israel.

Now David, too, wished to go to serve the king. But his father refused. "You are only a lad, little David. Of what help could you be to King Saul?"

And when David said again he wished to go to serve the king, his father again refused, saying, "Of all my sons, only you are left. And if you go, who will guard my sheep?"

"Father," said David, "the old shepherd at the next farm could guard your sheep along with his."

And again David said he wished to go to serve the king. And again his father refused, saying, "Little David, if you leave me, who will sing to me? Who will play on the harp to comfort me in my loneliness?" And the old man wept.

So David said no more, but played on his harp and sang a song to comfort his father. And the next morning David went once more to take his father's sheep to graze on the hillside.

David longed to serve the king. He was sure that, even though he was a lad, and a small one at that, he could be of service to his king and country. And he hoped that somehow he would find a way—or the Lord would show him a way—to serve the king. He would wait.

And while he was waiting, he watched his father's sheep and played on his harp and made up songs of praise.

Sometimes he wove a necklace of poppies for his favorite lamb, and a crown of poppies for himself. Then he would leap and dance and sing, "See, I am King David, King David with my crown. And the sheep are my subjects."

Then he would sigh. "I will never be even a soldier of the king, let alone a king myself!"

One day, just as evening was coming on and David was leading his sheep to shelter, a lion came and snatched up David's favorite lamb. David quickly put a stone in his slingshot and slung it at the lion. The lion was wounded, but still he did not let go of the lamb.

Though the lion was so big and David was so little, David ran up to the lion and struck him with his staff and snatched the lamb out of the lion's mouth.

Then the lion turned on David and would have killed him, surely, but David struck a mighty blow with his staff and killed the lion.

David skinned the lion and brought the lion skin to his father and told him all that had happened.

"It was the Lord," David said, "who gave me the courage and the strength. And now, surely, Father," David said, "I have shown that I can serve King Saul."

"Wait yet a little while," his father said.

Now just at this time, King Saul and his army were in great trouble. For the Philistines had gathered together their armies to battle. The Philistines stood on a mountain on the one side. King Saul and his men of Israel stood on a mountain on the other side, and there was a valley between them.

And each day there came into the valley a great giant who was a champion of the Philistines. The giant's name was Goliath of Gath. And each day he came out and called to the armies of Israel in a voice like thunder:

"Choose you a man for you and let him come down to me. If he be able to fight with me and to kill me, then all the Philistines will be your servants. But if I prevail against him and kill him, then all of you shall become our slaves and serve us."

When King Saul and all his men saw the great giant Goliath and heard these words, they were greatly afraid. No one in all the king's army dared to answer the giant's challenge.

Every day for forty days the giant Goliath of Gath came out and shouted his challenge in a voice like thunder. And every day King Saul and all his soldiers trembled with fear.

Now David and his father had no news of the army or of David's brothers who were there. And they knew nothing of the giant Goliath.

Every day David took his father's sheep to graze on the hillside, and every day David longed more than ever to serve in the king's army.

One day, not long after David had killed the lion, a great bear came among the flock. The sheep fled in terror, but David put a stone in his slingshot and slung it and killed the bear. Then David brought the bearskin to his father and once more begged leave to go to King Saul.

At last David's father said David could go to the army camp to bring back news of his brothers.

So David rose early the next morning and left the sheep in the care of the old shepherd who lived nearby.

David's father gave him ten loaves of bread and a measure of parched corn to take to his brothers. And he gave David ten cheeses as a gift for the captain of the army.

"Now run," David's father told him. "Run to the camp and come back quickly with news of your brothers."

Even as he hurried on his way, David was making a song of praise—a song praising the Lord:

"I will praise thee with my whole heart.
Before the gods will I sing praise unto thee.
I will praise thy name for thy loving kindness. . . .
In the day when I cried, thou answered me,
And strengthened me with strength in my soul. . . .
Though I walk in the midst of trouble, thou wilt revive me.
Thou shalt stretch forth thine hand against the wrath of mine enemies,
And thy right hand shall save me."

As David came to the camp, he heard great noise and shouting, for the armies of the Philistines and the armies of Israel were preparing to fight that day, army against army.

David left the bread and cheese and parched corn with a baggage keeper and ran to find his brothers, and he greeted them joyfully.

But David's brothers were not at all glad to see him. His eldest brother, Eliab, scolded him, "Why have you come here? Who is guarding the sheep? I know your pride. You have come to see the battle so you can boast of it."

Before David could answer, the great giant Goliath of Gath stepped out from the camp of the Philistines to challenge the army of Israel one last time.

"I defy the armies of Israel this day," he shouted in a voice like thunder. "Give me a man that we may fight together!"

And all the men of the army of Israel trembled with fear.

Then David asked some of the soldiers what the giant's challenge meant, and they told him. And they told him further, that to the man who killed the giant, the king would give great riches—and his daughter in marriage.

"But who among us," the soldiers added, "would dare to fight this giant?"

David looked out into the valley where the great giant Goliath of Gath was standing.

On the giant's head was a helmet of brass, and it shone in the sun like a second sun, so that David's eyes were dazzled. And the giant was armed with a great coat of mail. To protect the giant's legs, there were greaves of brass. His legs looked like two huge tree trunks covered with brass.

The giant Goliath carried a great spear. And the staff of the spear was like a weaver's beam.

David saw all this. Then he turned to the soldiers near him and said, "I shall fight the giant Goliath of Gath."

David's brothers were angry, for they thought this was the boast of a young and foolish lad, and they ordered David to return to his sheep.

But some other soldiers brought David before King Saul. And David bowed low before the king and said, "Let no man tremble because of the giant Goliath of Gath. I am here to serve you, and I will go and fight with this Philistine."

King Saul looked kindly at David and tried not to smile. "How can you fight this great giant?" asked the king. "You are only a lad and a shepherd. But Goliath of Gath is a mighty giant, and a soldier since his youth."

Then David said to the king, "It is true I am only a lad, and a small one at that. It is true I am only a shepherd and have no experience of arms. But one day as I was keeping my sheep, a lion came to take a lamb from my flock. And one day a bear came."

Then David told King Saul how he had killed both the lion and the bear. "And in the same way, I shall kill this Philistine giant," David said. "For my courage and my strength came from the Lord. And the Lord that delivered me out of the paw of the lion and out of the paw of the bear, He will deliver me out of the hand of this Philistine."

So at last King Saul gave his consent. "Go, and the Lord go with thee," he said. And he ordered his men to arm David with a helmet of shining brass and a coat of gleaming mail, and to gird him with a sword. A messenger was sent to the camp of the Philistines to tell Goliath that his challenge was accepted.

But when little David was clothed in all his heavy armor, he could not walk. So heavily did the armor weigh upon him, he could scarcely move. "I am only a shepherd boy," he said. "I cannot wear this armor. I cannot carry this sword." And David took them off—the helmet and the coat of mail and the sword.

And David took his staff in one hand, and chose him five smooth stones out of the brook and put them in the shepherd's bag that he carried over his shoulder.

Now, with his slingshot in his other hand, David went out to meet the Philistine giant, Goliath of Gath.

Goliath, too, walked out to meet his opponent. And a man walked before him to carry his shield.

But Goliath was so tall and David was so small that at first Goliath could not see the shepherd lad.

Goliath looked all around, and when he finally saw little David standing there with his shepherd's staff, the giant said, "Am I a dog, that you come after me with a stick?" Then Goliath laughed scornfully, and said in a voice like thunder:

"Come, come a little closer, and I will feed your flesh to the birds of the air and to the beasts of the field."

Then David said to the giant Goliath:

"You come with a sword and with a spear and with a shield. But I come in the name of the Lord, the God of the armies of Israel. And the Lord will deliver you into my hand, and I will strike you and kill you and cut off your head."

The giant gave a roar of anger and rushed at David to strike him with his sword.

David ran toward the giant. And as he ran, he put his hand in his shepherd's bag and took out a stone. Then he put the stone in his slingshot and slung it and struck the giant on the forehead.

And the giant Goliath of Gath fell with his face to the earth.

David ran and stood upon Goliath and took the giant's sword. Then David lifted the sword with both hands and cut off the giant's head.

A great cheer went up from the army of Israel. And when the Philistines saw that their champion was dead, they ran away.

So David brought the giant's head to King Saul. And King Saul would not let David return home, but he took him to his palace and brought him up as his own son.

Saul gave David gold and silver, and robes of linen and of finest wool.

And David fought for King Saul when there were battles to fight. And when King Saul was sad, David sang and played his harp to comfort him.

When David grew older, he married the king's daughter. And when Saul died, David became king, and he wore a crown of gold set with red rubies.